CONNECTION
BIBLE STUDY GUIDES

WORSHIP:

Life with Passion and Purpose

By Skip Heitzig

Companion Tape Series Available
FOR INFORMATION CALL
TOLL FREE 1-800-922-1888

CONNECTION
COMMUNICATIONS

Worship: Life with Passion and Purpose

Published by Connection Communications

ISBN 1-886324-34-4

Printed in the United States by Morris Publishing

3212 East Highway 30 • Kearney, NE 68847

1-800-650-7888

Table of Contents

With the Companion Tape Series:

WORSHIP:
Life with Passion and Purpose

You Are Invited to Worship
Psalm 95

Scripture is dominated by the theme of worship. One version of the Bible mentions the word *worship* four hundred times. In every book of the Bible, in every generation, people worshiped God. And from what the Bible tells us, worship is one of the chief activities of heaven (Rev. 5:9-14).

Psalm 95 is an invitation to worship. Through studying this invitation, we learn what it means to worship, and how worship can become a way of life that is both appropriate and fulfilling.

I. The Meaning of Worship: What Does it Imply? (v. 6)

Worship is a lifestyle of adoration in which we place God above everything and everyone else. Worship is not just an event, activity, or emotion.

A. **Worship Is a Response to God** (1 John 4:19).

B. **Worship Is a Response to God from Our Hearts** (John 4:23-24). We are told to worship "in spirit and truth."

C. **Worship Is the Proper Response Whereby We Place God Above Everything Else.** He is supremely worthy of worship (Deut. 6:5; Matt. 10:37; Rom. 12:1).

1. Worship means "to declare value or worth."
   a. Derived from the Old English word, *weorthscipe,* meaning "worthiness, respect."
   b. Shortened to "worshipe" (Middle English), then "worship."
2. Worship is not synonymous with praise.
   a. We worship God for who He is and who we are; we praise Him for what He does.
   b. Worship is ongoing; praise is episodic, in response to God's activities.

KEY THOUGHT

"Worship is the missing jewel of the evangelical church." — A.W. Tozer

II. The Motives for Worship: Why Should it Be Done?

We cannot give worship the priority it deserves until we understand and believe its importance.

A. **We Worship God Because of Who He Is.** God alone is worthy of our worship. He is the only one who can be described in the following terms.
   1. He is the Lord and the Rock of our salvation (v. 1).
   2. He is the great God, and the great King above all gods (v. 3).
   3. He is the Creator and Owner of earth and everything on it (v. 4-5).
   4. He is our Maker and our God (v. 6-7).
   5. He is a just God (v. 8-11).
   6. He is God the Son, Jesus Christ (Rev. 5:9).
      a. He was crucified to redeem us and restore our relationship with God.
      b. Christ's death and our salvation make the cross the center of all worship.
   7. He is the only God (Ex. 20:1-3).

8. He is a jealous God (Ex. 20:5).
9. He is our reason for existence (Col. 3:3).
10. He is above the angels (Rev. 19:10).

B. **We Worship God Because of Who We Are.** We exist because of Him and for Him and we worship Him because He is worth it. God's glory is the primary objective of worship. Any benefit we receive is secondary.

1. God owns us.
   a. We are His creation; He is the Creator (Gen. 1:26-28).
   b. We are His sheep; He is the Good Shepherd (John 10:11,14).
   c. We are His servants; He is our Lord (1 Cor. 4:1).
   d. He purchased us with His own Son's life (Acts 20:28).
   e. We choose to give our lives to Him (Matt. 10:39; Mark 8:35; Luke 9:24; John 12:25).
2. Worship is our natural response to God.
   a. A creature worships its creator (Col. 1:16; Rev. 4:11).
   b. Sheep dependently worship their shepherd.
   c. Subjects worship their sovereign lord.
   d. God's Son saved us so we could become worshipers.
   e. Worship is the natural, proper response from our hearts whereby we place God above everyone and everything else in our lives.

III. The Modes of Worship: How Should It Be Accomplished?

A. With Our Peers.

1. Psalm 95 is a call to public, corporate worship: "Let us..." (v. 1, 2, 6).

a. The Jews journeyed to Jerusalem three times a year for occasions of sacrifice, feasting, and corporate worship.
b. They journeyed together as families, as neighbors, as Jews.
c. As they journeyed, they worshiped together, reaffirming the faith that brought them together and called them to make these journeys.

2. Corporate worship encourages and inspires each of us on our own journey of faith.
3. Corporate worship is commanded in Scripture (Heb. 10:25).
4. Corporate worship is taught by Jesus: "Our Father...give us this day our daily bread..." (Matt. 6:9-13).

B. With Our Lips.

1. God's Word tells us to "sing" and "shout joyfully" in worship (v. 1, 2; 98:4, 6).
2. God created us with voices so we can use them to worship Him.
3. God also gives us the joy from which our worship should come.
   a. Even when we are discouraged, God is worthy of our worship.

C. With Our Bodies.

1. Bowing down (v. 6).
2. Kneeling (v. 6).
3. Raising our hands (1 Tim. 2:8).

D. With Our Lives.

1. We worship God by obeying Him.
2. Israel worshiped God corporately with their voices, but they did not worship God with their daily lives.

3. True worship is the lifestyle of a life transformed through a relationship with God. We shouldn't only talk about transformation—we should exhibit it!

Scripture tells us that one day every knee will bow and every tongue will confess Jesus Christ as Lord. Until then, each day is an opportunity to rehearse for that day—and an opportunity to impact others as they see our lifestyle of contagious worship.

1. How closely does your worship resemble the biblical description of worship? Assessing all your activities and interests in life, is it accurate to say you worship God? Does your life seem to revolve around you or does your life revolve around God and His interests?

2. Why is it appropriate to worship even when life comes crashing down on you?

3. How does corporate worship change your perspective?

Why Are You Here?

Matthew 21:12-17

When we go to a doctor's office, we're often asked a typical question: "So, what brings you here?" Our answers may range from a sore throat to something far more serious. Similarly, if each of us was asked why we go to church, our answers would vary widely.

Why are we here? It's a good question to ask. Jeremiah wrote, "Let us search out and examine our ways..." (Lam. 3:40). Paul said, "For if we would judge ourselves, we would not be judged" (1 Cor. 11:31).

Jesus was in Jerusalem the day after his triumphal entry. The season was Passover and an estimated 2.5 million people were in Jerusalem at that time—five times the city's normal population. The temple was the focal point of worship. While Jesus was in the temple, he encountered four groups of people there for four very different reasons. He responded to each group in accordance with their response to Him.

I. The Self-Seeking (v. 12–13).

Some came as opportunists. They came with their hands out to *work* and *get*, not *worship* and *give*. Jesus drove them out.

A. The Background.

1. Jesus had encountered exploitation of the temple before (John 2:14-15).
2. The Jewish high priest sold rights to merchants allowing them to sell goods for sacrifice and exchange money for offerings on temple property.

3. These merchants charged a premium for their goods and services.
    a. The merchants and priests told people their sacrifice was unworthy, then sold them a new sacrifice for up to ten times its worth.
    b. Foreigners needing to exchange foreign money for temple shekels were charged a 25 percent surcharge.
    c. The high priest received a portion of the merchants' profits.
4. This has happened throughout history.
    a. The church sold indulgences during medieval times.
    b. So-called religious organizations solicit offerings through mail, television, and other means, promising some form of blessing in exchange.

B. Jesus' Response.

1. Jesus' response was intense.
    a. Jesus drove them out of the temple (v. 12).
    b. Jesus does not tolerate feigned worship—worship of self in the name of God.
    c. God never separates worship from the worshipers.
2. Jesus' response was scriptural (v. 13).
    a. Jesus explained His actions by quoting Isaiah 56:7.
    b. In our worship and in our lives, the best rule of thumb is to ask ourselves what the Bible says. Everything we do should be based on and defensible by God's Word.
    c. Peter used Scripture to explain the disciples speaking in tongues on the day of Pentecost (Acts 2:15-21; Joel 2:28-32).
3. Jesus' response was driven by the glory of God.

a. God's house exists for His glory (Isa. 56:7).
b. These people were taking advantage of people's heartfelt desire to worship.
c. Those who desire to use God's house for personal gain are attempting to steal glory that belongs to God alone.

II. The Genuinely Hurting.

Some came to the temple with their heads hung low in genuine need and brokenness. Jesus met their needs (v. 14).

A. The People. People with physical, social, and emotional needs typically hung out around the temple.
1. Jews of that time believed that any physical abnormality was a judgment from God in response to a person's sin.
2. Those with abnormalities were ignored, mocked, and often forced to beg for daily sustenance.
3. Passover brought many of these people to the temple with hopes of receiving a small amount of money from merciful temple-goers.

B. Their Intent. They came to Jesus, not just the temple: "The blind and the lame came to Him in the temple" (v. 14).
1. The moneychangers were fixed on the place of the temple because it was a place of opportunity.
2. Those in need were fixed on the person, Jesus Christ. They came to the temple because Jesus was there.
   a. They made no demands, and they had no ulterior motives.
   b. They simply came with their needs.

C. **Jesus' Response.** Jesus met them where they were and changed their conditon, responding with life-transforming healing.

1. God is in the restoration business. He knows us and understands our needs (Ps. 103:14).
2. Jesus came to meet the needs of those who are broken (Isa. 61:1; Luke 4:18).
3. We all have needs, and need is often what will drive a person back to Christ.
   a. God is all about change. He gave sight to the blind, and made the lame to walk.
   b. Some people may feel overlooked by the crowd. Jesus sees their need and meets them there.

What do you need today? God is waiting for you to come to Him. He's waiting to transform your life.

III. The Piously Resenting (v. 15–17).

Some came to the temple with clenched fists and hardened hearts: "The chief priests and scribes...were indignant" (v. 15). Jesus left them.

A. The Leaders.

1. The chief priests were professional clergy. They were in charge of the worship at the temple and the sacrifices.
2. The scribes were the scholars of Scripture. They spent their time copying the law.
3. These leaders were present in the temple daily. They participated in its services and prayed its prayers, but they were untouched by the power and presence of Jesus Christ.
   a. They were arrogant and hardened.
   b. Paul warned the Galatians against developing this attitude (Gal. 3:2-3).

c. Many people walk the road of academia, and the more they handle spiritual things, the more into form and further from Jesus Christ they get.

Jesus comforts the afflicted who come to Him in need. He afflicts the comfortable who approach Him with arrogance.

KEY THOUGHT

B. **Jesus' Response.** Jesus again responded with Scripture and action (v. 16-17).

1. He quoted Scripture (v. 16; Ps. 8:2).
   a. He came to them on their level.
   b. They were not persuaded; God's Word did not penetrate their hearts.
2. He left—perhaps the saddest response of all (v. 17).
   a. He drove out the moneychangers.
   b. He drove disease out of the blind and lame.
   c. With those angry hypocrites with spiritual masks, He himself left.
3. God never separates worship from the worshiper.
   a. Abel's offering was accepted; Cain's was not (Gen. 4:4-5).
   b. Like the chief priest and scribes, Cain was angry (Gen. 4:5).
   c. God rejected Cain's offering because his heart was not right.
      i. Cain was not worshiping with a heart of obedience.
      ii. If the heart of the worshiper is corrupt, then the gift is corrupt and unacceptable to God (Gen. 4:7).

d. Abel brought to God the best he could bring—the firstborn of the flock, but there is no mention of the quality of Cain's gift. (Gen. 4:4).
e. Similarly, David insisted on paying for a field he intended to use for God's temple (1 Chron. 21:18-25).
f. Many people wrongly think that God is content with our merely attending church.
g. The personal value of our offering—whether assets, abilities, or availability—indicates the condition of our heart toward God.

IV. The Simply Adoring (v. 15b, 16b).

Some came to the temple with open hands and hearts overflowing with praise. Jesus praised them.

A. **The People.** The word in Greek is *pais,* literally meaning "boys." They were likely teenage boys (v. 15).

B. **Their Action.** They cried out to Jesus in spontaneous praise: "Hosanna!" (v. 15).
   1. Their praise wasn't intellectual or lengthy.
   2. Their praise was from their hearts.

C. **Jesus' Response.** Jesus responded with approval: He called their worship "perfect" (v. 16; Ps. 8:2). Their worship was an appropriate response to God from their hearts. In it, they placed God above everything else in their lives.

How do you worship? If you come into God's presence merely for a handout, hear His rebuke. If you come with a broken heart, feel His healing embrace. If you come with an angry, self-filled heart, see His turned back. If you come with a heart filled with praise for God alone, receive His affirmation of the perfection of your praise.

1. Some people come to God with their hands out (when they want something); others approach Him when they are in pain and need a touch (their hands are hung low); and others revel in a skin-deep religious display, without being genuinely changed (they look at others angrily with clenched fists); still others come with raised hands, simply and spontaneously adoring Him. Which of the above best describes you?
2. Can one person's worship include elements of all four approaches? How could a person change from one approach to another?
3. Notice again Jesus' four responses to the varied approaches: anger, healing, leaving, and approval. How does God manifest these today?

Worship: True or False?

John 4:20-24

The world is full of worshipers. The desire to worship is built into us by God. Yet, it could accurately be said to many who claim to worship, "You worship what you do not know" (John 4:22).

What worship does God desire? Does He consider all worship true worship? In Jesus' encounter with the Samaritan woman at the well, we find insight into what true worship looks like, and what worship God sees as false.

I. Confusion Concerning Worship.

Sin and lifelong habits and beliefs can confuse us about what worship truly is.

- **A. Due to Sin.** Sin skews our view and taints our worship of God.
  1. The woman had a sinful past: She had been divorced several times and was now living with a man who was not her husband (v. 18).
     - a. She was hard and pessimistic.
     - b. When Jesus spoke of living water, her answer was cynical and suspicious. She had been around many men and did not trust them.
  2. Jesus told her He knew of her sin (v. 17-18).
     - a. He knew her sin was the core of her confusion about God.
     - b. He knew she was blinded to her sin and needed to acknowledge it.
  3. She responded first with awe, then with discomfort.

   a. She perceived Jesus was a prophet because of what He knew about her (v. 19).
   b. She changed the subject to a larger, less personal topic that allowed her to criticize someone else (v. 20).
4. Sin obscures our view of God and how He is to be worshiped.
5. Until we deal with sin, our worship is unacceptable to God.
6. The woman wanted to worship God—she asked Jesus to "give me this water" (v. 15), but her sin stood in the way.

B. Confusion Due to Background. A look at this woman's background reveals that she was religious—at least in her upbringing. Lifelong tradition can hold us back from embracing life-giving truth.

1. As a Samaritan, this woman had been raised to oppose the Jews (v. 7).
   a. In 722 B.C., the Assyrian Empire captured the Jews in Samaria and repopulated Samaria with foreigners.
   b. The foreigners brought in their own gods but also began worshiping the God of the Jews.
   c. As a result of this infiltration of Samaria, the Jews of Jerusalem refused to associate with Samaritan Jews.
   d. When the Samaritans offered to help rebuild the temple after its Babylonian destruction, the Jews of Jerusalem rejected their help because of the corruption in their worship.
2. Her knowledge of God was limited.
   a. In response to the Jews' rejection, the Samaritans built their own temple, revised

some of the Bible's stories, and acknowledged only the first five books of Moses.

3. Her understanding of worship was imperfect.
4. Many of us have been raised within some sort of cultural or religious framework.
   a. Because traditions and beliefs become so infused in our lives, they are hard to break.
   b. When our framework is wrong, its stronghold on our life can keep us from true relationship with, and worship of, God.

KEY THOUGHT

The difference between standing still and moving forward spiritually is obedience to our heavenly Father. When God becomes the center of your life—when His will overshadows your will and His ways are more predominant than yours—you will have discovered the essence of true worship.

II. Clarity Concerning Worship.

True worship is relational, informed, authentic, and all about God.

A. True Worship Cannot Be Confined to a Place (v. 20-21).

1. The Bible tells us several times God cannot be confined to a place.
   a. Jesus told the woman at the well: "The hour is coming when you will neither on this mountain, nor in Jerusalem, worship the Father" (v. 21).
   b. Solomon told the Jews at the dedication of the temple: "Behold, heaven and the heaven of heavens cannot contain You. How much less this temple which I have built!" (2 Chron. 6:18).

   c. Stephen told the Jewish elders: "The Most High does not dwell in temples made with hands" (Acts 7:48).
2. Many people have traveled to specific places hoping to have extraordinary experiences.
   a. Ten million people traveled to Medjugorje, Yugoslavia, in hope of seeing the Virgin Mary.
   b. Each year 2 million Muslims travel to Mecca because Mohammed said they should do so.
   c. Every Good Friday, hundreds of thousands travel to El Santuario de Chimayo for holy, healing dirt.
   d. Many Christians travel to Israel with the expectation that God will meet them there and impact their faith in an extraordinary way.
3. God sometimes meets us in special ways in the midst of very ordinary circumstances.
4. Our proximity and ability to worship God is measured in relationship, not miles.
   a. A person may have a great spiritual experience in a certain place, and from that point look to that place for another experience.
   b. In Jeremiah 23, God says: "'Am I a God who is only in one place?' asks the Lord. '...Can anyone hide from me? Am I not everywhere in all the heavens and earth?' asks the Lord" (Jer. 23:23-24 NLT).
   c. Being near or far to God is not a question of space but of spirit. A life intertwined with Jesus' can't get any closer.

B. True Worship Must Have the Right Basis. True worshipers worship God in spirit and truth (v. 23).

1. Samaritan worship was spirit without truth (v. 22).
    a. They only accepted the first five books of Moses so their knowledge of God was limited.
    b. Their worship was that of zeal without knowledge.
2. The Jews worshiped God in truth without spirit.
    a. They thoroughly studied and practiced the truths they read in all thirty-nine books of the Old Testament.
    b. They went through the motions of worship but their hearts were not in it. They had grown cold, legalistic, and empty.
    c. Jesus said of the Jews, "These people draw near to Me with their mouth, and honor Me with their lips, but their heart is far from Me" (Matt. 15:8).

C. What Does It Mean to Worship God in Spirit?

1. "In spirit" refers to the human spirit, not the Holy Spirit.
    a. If Jesus had been referring to the Holy Spirit, He would have said "in the Spirit," rather than, "in spirit."
    b. The human spirit is the core, the heart of a person.
    c. The apostle Paul said, "God...whom I serve with my spirit" (Rom. 1:9).
2. To worship God in spirit, we need the Holy Spirit living in us.
    a. We must have relationship with Christ in order for His Spirit to be living in us. Paul said, "For we are the circumcision, who worship God in the Spirit, rejoice in Christ Jesus, and have no confidence in the flesh" (Phil 3:3).

   b. The Holy Spirit, who lives in us, prompts us to worship.
3. To worship God in spirit, we must focus our thoughts.
   a. God wants us to come to Him prepared and committed to worship from the core of who we are.
   b. God wants us to come to Him expecting Him to respond. Jesus said, "Ask, and it will be given to you; seek, and you will find; knock, and it will be opened to you" (Matt. 7:7).
   c. God said the Old Testament priests "despised My Name" because of their attitude toward worship (Mal. 1:6).

D. What Does It Mean To Worship God in Truth?

1. For worship to be valid, it must be based on the Word of God. Of the Jews, Jesus said, "We know what we worship" (v. 22).
2. God tells us in His Word how He wants to be worshiped. Psalm 47:7 tells us, "For God is the King of all the earth; sing praises with understanding."
3. God rejects worship that is not done in truth.
   a. Aaron and the children of Israel made a golden calf and worshiped it; for that, God judged them (Ex. 32).
   b. Nadab and Abihu offered profane fire before the Lord in the Wilderness of Sinai"; God took their lives (Num. 3:4).
   c. Saul, too impatient to wait for the prophet Samuel to offer the sacrifices, offered them himself; God shortened Saul's reign over Israel (1 Sam. 13:8-14).
   d. Uzzah, a bearer of the Ark of the Covenant, departed from the instructions

given by God. "God struck him there for his error; and he died there by the ark of God" (2 Sam. 6:3-7).

e. The Pharisees rebuked Jesus for breaking a tradition that didn't come from God's Word; Jesus rebuked them for developing a tradition that wasn't based on Scripture (Matt. 15:1-11).

E. True Worship Must Have the Right Object.

1. True worshipers worship God the Father (v. 21, 23).
   a. They worship God for who and all He is.
   b. They worship God and only God (Ex. 20:2-5a).
2. False worshipers give humans the credit for all God has done.

Scripture tells us God is actively, earnestly seeking true worshipers who will worship Him in spirit and in truth (John 4:23). Has God found a true worshiper in you? Are you one who worships only Him from the core of your being, the way His Word tells you to, any place at any time, with nothing obscuring your view of Him?

1. What two elements bring proper balance to our worship? Describe the role of both of these in your own experience.

2. Read Psalm 51:15-17. What things does God desire in our worship?

3. How has your personal upbringing and understanding clouded your view of true, biblical worship?

Lift Up Your Voice, Part 1

Psalm 47

Somehow, a large number of churchgoers have bought into the idea that "singing in church is only for people with good voices." Wrong! Singing is for believers! The words *sing, sang,* and *song* are mentioned 206 times throughout the Bible. Therefore, the question is not, "Do you have a good voice?" but rather, "Do you have a song?"

Singing is a part of history: spiritually, culturally, and socially. We work to music, drive to it, and wait in offices to it. It's a prominent part of humanity. More than that it will occupy an important place in our future. Remember: God is not auditioning us—He's conditioning us for the future. So clear your throat and get in practice—for eternity!

I. Singing Is Prominent in the Past.

From God's first creation to His chosen people, the past has given us a legacy of song.

A. **At Creation.** God's creation is naturally compelled to respond to Him with song.

1. God asked Job, "Where were you when I laid the foundations of the earth? ... When the morning stars sang together, and all the sons of God shouted for joy?" (Job 38:4, 7).
2. Isaiah prophesied, "The mountains and the hills shall break forth into singing before You, and all the trees of the field shall clap their hands" (Isa. 55:12).

3. Jesus told the Pharisees, "I tell you that if these [disciples] should keep silent, the stones would immediately cry out" (Luke 19:40).

B. **During Sacrifice.** God's people responded with song to God's forgiveness of their sins.
   1. Israel worshiped God with song as He accepted the blood sacrifices for their sins (2 Chron. 29:20-30).
      a. They worshiped with instruments: "with cymbals, with stringed instruments, and with harps ... and the priests with the trumpets" (2 Chron. 29:25-26).
      b. They worshiped with song: "So they sang praises with gladness, and they bowed their heads and worshiped" (2 Chron. 29:30).
   2. Our redemption through Jesus' blood is worth singing about.

KEY THOUGHT

> "For music is a gift in the grace of God, not the invention of men. Thus it drives out the Devil, and it makes people cheerful. Then one forgets all wrath, impurity, and other devices."
> — Martin Luther

C. **On the Battlefield.**
   1. Jehoshaphat "appointed those who should sing to the Lord ... as they went out before the army..." (2 Chron. 20:21).
      a. It encouraged the troops.
      b. It glorified God: "...and [they] were saying: 'Praise the LORD, for His mercy endures forever'" (2 Chron. 20:21).
      c. It defeated the enemy: "When they began to sing and to praise, the LORD set ambushes against the people of Ammon, Moab, and Mount Seir...and they were defeated" (2 Chron. 20:22).

2. Deborah, a judge of Israel, sang a song celebrating Israel's victory on the battlefield: "Hear, O kings! Give ear, O princes! I, even I, will sing to the LORD; I will sing praise to the LORD God of Israel" (Judges 5:3).

D. For the Feasts.

1. The Book of Psalms was Israel's songbook for their feasts.
2. For the arrival of the Ark of the Covenant in Jerusalem, David told the Levites to assemble a group to "be the singers accompanied by instruments of music, stringed instruments, harps, and cymbals, by raising the voice with resounding joy" (1 Chron. 15:16-28).
3. Singing was a part of the Passover meal. Jesus sang the *Hallel* at the Passover meal before His death: "And when they had sung a hymn, they went out to the Mount of Olives" (Matt. 26:30; Mark 14:26).
4. Singing to God became a vocation for Israel.
   a. At the Festival of First Fruits, they sang of God's provision for them.
   b. At the Passover, they sang of God's redemption of them.
   c. Each Sabbath, they sang in celebration of God's creation.

II. Singing Is Prescribed in the Present.

The New Testament tells us what to sing, when and how to sing, and what can happen when God's people sing.

A. The Church's Example. From the beginning, the early church modeled singing to Jesus.

B. Paul's Instructions. Paul encouraged singing between Christians, and from Christians to God.

1. Sing as a way of life: "...be filled with the Spirit, speaking to one another in psalms and hymns and spiritual songs, singing and making melody in your heart to the Lord" (Eph. 5:18b-19).
2. Sing to convey and celebrate truth: "Let the word of Christ dwell in you richly in all wisdom, teaching and admonishing one another in psalms and hymns and spiritual songs, singing with grace in your hearts to the Lord" (Col. 3:16).

C. **James' Instructions.** James instructed singing to express and share joy: "Is anyone cheerful? Let him sing psalms" (Jas. 5:13).
1. Singing conveys truth to those who hear it: "Paul and Silas were praying and singing hymns to God, and the prisoners were listening to them" (Acts 16:25).
2. Singing can save lives: "The keeper of the prison...fell down trembling before Paul and Silas. And he brought them out and said, 'Sirs, what must I do to be saved?'" (Acts 16:27-30).
3. Singing in the midst of oppression demonstrates maturity of faith.

Don't face life's battles alone. Bring God to work, into your family, and to all the places where you fight the battles of life. Raise the shield of God's faithfulness by lifting your voice in song.

III. Singing Is Predicted in the Future.

All of heaven and earth will praise God with singing (Rev. 5:13).

A. **The Occupants of Heaven** (Rev. 5:8-14).

1. The occupants of heaven include "many angels around the throne, the living creatures, and the elders" (v. 11).
2. They will sing as a multitude: "The number of them was ten thousand times ten thousand, and thousands of thousands" (v. 11).
3. They will sing "with a loud voice" (v. 12).
4. They will sing to the Lamb, Jesus Christ (v. 8).
5. They will sing "a new song" to celebrate God's victory over Satan, the full redemption of God's creation: "You are worthy to take the scroll, and to open its seals; for You were slain, and have redeemed us to God by Your blood" (v. 9).
    a. At creation, there was song.
    b. At the redemption of creation, there will be song.
    c. As we await the redemption event, we, God's creation, should be in song.

KEY THOUGHT

God gave humans alone the choice to worship Him. The rest of God's creation worships Him naturally, instinctively, continuously. When we choose not to worship Him, we live at a lower level than the mountains, trees, rocks, and animals.

B. The Occupants of Earth (Rev. 14, 15).

1. One hundred and forty-four thousand Jews will sing (Rev. 14).
    a. They will bear the "Father's name written on their foreheads" (v. 1; Rev. 7:4).
    b. They will sing "a new song...no one could learn...except the hundred and forty-four thousand who were redeemed from the earth" (v. 3).

   c. All of the number sealed by God before the Tribulation will be there at the end to sing to Him.
2. The martyrs of the Tribulation will sing (Rev. 15).
   a. Tortured for their faith in Jesus Christ, they have received "victory over the beast, over his image and over his mark and over the number of his name" (v. 2).
   b. They will sing "the song of Moses, the servant of God, and the song of the Lamb, saying: 'Great and marvelous are Your works, Lord God Almighty! Just and true are Your ways, O King of the saints'" (v. 3).
3. If these survivors of tribulation can sing praises to God for His justice and truth, we, too, can sing to God despite the pain in our lives.
   a. Some people respond to pain with bitterness and anger toward God.
   b. Some people respond to pain with resignation and withdrawal from God.
   c. Some people respond to pain with tenacious trust and an ongoing song of praise.

It's one thing to profess belief in, commitment to, and love for God. It's another to live as though He really exists, has everything under control, and will sovereignly ensure "that all things work together for good" (Rom. 8:28). Worship in song is the appropriate, natural response from the heart of someone who loves and trusts God above everyone and everything else.

1. This week, think of your favorite psalm and make up your own melody.

2. Memorize a song to sing when you suffer. Develop the habit of expressing your faith to God even at times when everything around you is bleak.

Lift Up Your Voice, Part 2

Ephesians 5:19

Songs are everywhere. In almost every culture and country, music and singing leave their mark. Singing is the oldest form of music making. The first instrument ever used was the voice. Adding words to melody and music heightens their effect and makes them more memorable.

Singing is also a main component of worship. Every time God's people gather, they spend time singing the truth they believe. But what makes our singing different from a simple folk song or an anthem? Is it a time-filler for latecomers or merely a Christianized form of entertainment? Or is it something much deeper and significant?

I remember the first time I encountered true worshipers. Not yet a Christian, I watched the people around me. Some of them had their eyes closed or hands raised. A few swayed back and forth a little. I thought, "Uh oh. This is weird." I became uncomfortable and a little embarrassed. Why? Because they were in touch with Someone I wasn't yet in touch with. They knew something I didn't yet know. They were worshiping in spirit and in truth.

I. Why Should We Sing? (v. 15-19)

We should sing because we have a living song inside us.

A. Singing Is a Consequence of a Spirit-Filled Life. If God's Spirit lives in us, He puts a song in our hearts.

1. Being filled with the Spirit means having a singing heart: "Be filled with the Spirit, speaking to one another in psalms and hymns and

spiritual songs, singing and making melody in your heart to the Lord" (Eph. 5:18b-19).

2. Being filled with the Spirit is an ongoing, active condition.
3. Being filled with the Spirit means being controlled by, supplied with, and occupied with the Spirit. As the Spirit moves inside us, we respond through our actions.
4. Being filled with the Spirit means literally being filled up with God's Spirit. Everything the Spirit-filled person does is an outpouring of what is inside.
5. Being filled with the Spirit is deeply relational and produces powerful results. "[Jesus cried out], 'He who believes in Me, as the Scripture has said, out of his heart will flow rivers of living water.' But this He spoke concerning the Spirit, whom those believing in Him would receive..." (John 7:38-39).

B. **Singing Is Evidence of God's Word in Our Lives.** As God's Word enters our lives, He wants us to express it in song: "Let the word of Christ dwell in you richly in all wisdom, teaching and admonishing one another in psalms and hymns and spiritual songs, singing with grace in your hearts to the Lord" (Col. 3:16).

1. Being filled with the Spirit is closely related to knowing and obeying Scripture.
   a. The Holy Spirit authored the Bible.
   b. Greater understanding of Scripture allows the Holy Spirit to more effectively direct our lives.
2. The Reformation brought music back into the church because it also brought the Scriptures back.

a. For hundreds of years the church body didn't sing. They were sung to by choirs.
b. The Reformation changed that, bringing back the Bible and song.
c. Hymns embodied theology—doctrines of sin and redemption. The songs reinforced these ideas.

II. Who Should Sing?

God's people should sing to Him together.

A. Singing Is a *One-Another* Activity. "I will praise the Lord with my whole heart, in the assembly of the upright and in the congregation" (Ps. 111:1).

1. Singing to God should be done with "one another." We should:
   a. Prefer one another (Rom. 12:10).
   b. Edify one another (Rom. 14:19; 1 Thess. 5:11).
   c. Receive one another (Rom. 15:7).
   d. Admonish one another (Rom. 15:14).
   e. Greet one another (Rom. 16:16; 1 Cor. 16:20; 2 Cor. 13:12; 1 Pet. 5:14).
   f. Care for one another (1 Cor. 12:25).
   g. Serve one another (Gal. 5:13).
   h. Bear one another's burdens (Gal. 6:2).
   i. Forebear and forgive one another (Eph. 4:32; Col. 3:13).
   j. Submit to one another (Eph. 5:21; 1 Pet. 5:5).
   k. Comfort one another (1 Thess. 4:18, 5:11).
   l. Exhort one another (Heb. 3:13, 10:25).
   m. Consider one another (Heb. 10:24).
   n. Confess your faults to one another; pray for one another (Jas. 5:16).
   o. Minister gifts to one another (1 Pet. 4:10).

III. Why Should We Sing?

A. Singing Together Rebuilds What the World Erodes.

1. The world challenges our faith and wears us down. At the end of a week, our spiritual edge can be dulled.
2. When we sing together, we are refreshed. We are reminded of truth and reinforced in God's values.

B. Singing Together Refocuses What the World Blurs.

1. The world's messages try to drown out God's truth and make us feel alone, confused, and outnumbered.
2. Singing together reminds us that we're not alone and we're on the right track.

Afraid to show emotion toward the living God because you might be labeled by others? Go ahead. Get labeled. You are already: You're a Christian.

IV. What Should We Sing?

There are three categories of things we should sing: psalms, hymns, and spiritual songs. Singing to God together produces unique results.

A. Psalms.

1. The book of Psalms was the Jewish songbook. It later became the songbook of the early church.
2. There are one hundred fifty psalms to choose from.
3. They were mostly chants. The melodies were diatonic scales with a mix of quarter notes in the mid-eastern tradition.
4. They used *monophony,* an "emphasis on the beauty of the melody line itself." A single

strand of melody would be repeated multiple times.

5. Many psalms have been incorporated into hymns and contemporary worship songs.
   a. *A Mighty Fortress Is Our God* by Martin Luther is from Psalm 46.
   b. *Our God, Our Help in Ages Past* by Isaac Watts is from Psalm 90.

B. Hymns.

1. Hymns were probably written by the early church. They were principally about the work of Jesus Christ.
2. Scholars believe the New Testament includes portions of early Christian hymns.
   a. "Awake, you who sleep, Arise from the dead, And Christ will give you light" (Eph. 5:14).
   b. "God was manifested in the flesh, Justified in the Spirit, Seen by angels, Preached among the Gentiles, Believed on in the world, Received up in glory" (1 Tim. 3:16).

C. Spiritual Songs.

1. This is a general term. The intent is to give latitude and freedom to musical expression.
2. Every generation must have the freedom to write its own spiritual songs to express God's work.
3. In the Bible, the word "new" appears more often in connection with song than with any other single element.
4. Many of the songs we know today as "hymns" were controversial when first written.
   a. Martin Luther wrote hymns to the melodies of popular bar melodies.
   b. Isaac Watts began writing his own songs because he found the hymns of his time dull.

V. How Should We Sing?

You can sing speak or sing, but whatever you do should come from your heart.

A. In Our Hearts.

1. Translated one way, this could mean we are to keep our melody and God's grace inside our hearts; we should sing with our hearts but not our voices.
2. Translated another way, we are to sing from the depths of our hearts and with our entire hearts the song that has been put there by the Holy Spirit; we should sing with our hearts *and* our voices.
   a. David wrote multiple times, "I will praise You with my whole heart" (Ps. 9:1; 111:1; 138:1).
   b. In contrast, the Pharisees worshiped with their lips but not their voices (Matt. 15:8; Mark 7:6).
3. Singing in worship is meant to be intimate and genuine.
   a. The Greek word used in the New Testament to refer to worship, *proskuneo*, means "to kiss toward one in token of reverence."
   b. Intimacy and reverence require heartfelt passion and emotion.
4. At church services, some people seem to bubble over and glow, while others just exist. There is no real sense of celebration.
   a. You don't need to be a hyper, giddy person, but the Holy Spirit in a person produces a passionate life.
   b. Some people are embarrassed to show any emotion for things of God. There is nothing wrong with true excitement for the things of God.

VI. To Whom Should We Sing?

Before the Reformation, church choirs sang and the congregation listened. The average person didn't understand or participate in worship. Now the congregation has become the choir, with God as the sole audience. The motive of worship is to bless the Lord (Ps. 34).

Step your life up to a higher voltage, spiritually. Lift your heart and voice up without shame to God. If there's a song in your heart, let it out with joy and don't hold back. If your heart is songless, invite God today to fill your heart with His Spirit, song and "rivers of living water."

1. If worship steps life up to a higher voltage, how's your battery?
2. Take some time this week to charge yourself up in worship.

Abraham: Worship on Display

Genesis 18 and 22

Studying the subject of worship is one thing; seeing it in action is another. God has provided us with opportunity to do both through His Word. As we've studied already, the Bible tells us why, how, and Who to worship. As we'll discover today, God's Word also contains examples for us to follow.

When we're exhausted and disheartened from being pushed and pulled by the world, there's nothing like the worshipers in Scripture to inspire us to reconnect with God in worship. Like us, these people were misunderstood by those around them. In fact, the Bible describes them as people "of whom the world was not worthy" (Heb. 11:38).

Yet, when we glimpse their lives and see their worship displayed, we discover the kind of worship that's acceptable to God—and the effect it can have on our lives. Through three different cameos, Abraham's life shows us what true worship involves.

I. Worship Involves Service (Gen. 18:1-8).

As God's servants, our role is to worship Him through service.

- **A. Abraham Served God Intently.** As a servant, Abraham served his Lord intensely.
  1. The Lord appeared to Abraham in a special place (v. 1).
     - a. He appeared at the terebinth trees of Mamre, where Abraham had built an altar to God and worshiped.

b. He appeared in the heat of the day. People usually weren't traveling during this time.
c. This appearance is called a *theophany*: "A physical manifestation of God, usually referring to an appearance of Christ in human form."
d. The New Testament tells us angels still appear to people today: "Do not forget to entertain strangers, for by so doing some have unwittingly entertained angels" (Heb. 13:2).

2. Abraham saw the Lord and ran to Him. He recognized and worshiped Him (v. 2).
   a. Gen. 18:2 contains the first occurrence in the Bible of the Hebrew word *shachah*, which is translated as "worship" in the English language.
   b. *Shachah* appears more than one hundred times in Scripture.
   c. It means "to bow down, to prostrate oneself" (Brown, Driver, Briggs, Gesenius Lexicon).
   d. *Shachah* was the term used to describe a person's actions when meeting royalty.
3. Abraham served the Lord personally.
   a. He did not send a servant to wait on the Lord; he called himself "Your servant" v. 3).
   b. He begged God to be allowed to serve Him.
4. Abraham responded quickly, despite his aged condition.
   a. He "ran from the tent door to meet them" (v. 2).
   b. He "hurried into the tent" (v. 6).
   c. He said to Sarah, "Quickly, make ..." (v. 6).
   d. He "hastened to prepare" meat for his guests (v. 7).

5. Abraham gave the Lord his very best.
    a. He had Sarah "make ready three measures of fine meal; knead it and make cakes" (v. 6).
    b. He "took a tender and good calf...and hastened to prepare it" (v. 7).
    c. He also "took butter and milk" (v. 8).

B. **Abraham Worshiped and Served God.** Serving God is an act of worship.
1. Abraham both served and worshiped the Lord under the terebinth trees.
    a. Abraham built an altar there and worshiped God (Gen. 13:18).
    b. The Lord came to Abraham there (v. 1).
    c. Abraham responded by worshiping through serving (v. 3-8).
    d. Abraham took the worship of the altar home with him (v. 3-8).
2. Worship and service appear interchangeably in Scripture. This is clearly seen in Romans 12:1 which is translated two ways:
    a. "I urge you, brothers, in view of God's mercy, to offer your bodies as living sacrifices, holy and pleasing to God—this is your spiritual act of worship" (NIV).
    b. "I beseech you therefore, brethren, by the mercies of God, that you present your bodies a living sacrifice, holy, acceptable to God, which is your reasonable service" (NKJV)
    c. Jesus said, "You shall *worship* the Lord your God, and Him only you shall *serve*"(Matt. 4:10; Luke 4:8 emphasis added).

C. **Maturity Brings Service.** A natural spiritual progression moves us from receiving to wanting to give.

1. Stage One: Salvation.
   a. First we receive the gift of God's mercy and grace.
   b. God begins to work within us.
   c. We become hungry for more knowledge about Christ, our relationship with Him, and our relationship with His family.
2. Stage Two: Service.
   a. Realizing how much we have received, we develop the desire to give back to God, His church, and others who have blessed us.
   b. We read Scripture that tells us to serve, and we want to respond.
      i. Jesus said, "It is more blessed to give than to receive" (Acts. 20:35).
      ii. James tells us, "Be doers of the word, and not hearers only, deceiving yourselves" (Jas. 1:22).
      iii. Jesus said we serve Him whenever we serve others: "Inasmuch as you did it to one of the least of these My brethren, you did it to Me" (Matt. 25:40).
   c. When we respond in worship through serving, God is working through us.

KEY THOUGHT

Action without adoration leads to aggravation.

II. Worship Involves Solitude (Genesis 18:16-22).

When we withdraw from the world to spend time with God, He accepts this as worship.

A. **Abraham Was God's Friend.** As a friend, Abraham stood quietly before His Lord.
  1. Three times Scripture mentions Abraham specifically as God's friend.
     a. "...Abraham Your friend forever" (2 Chron. 20:7).
     b. "...Abraham My friend" (Isa. 41:8).
     c. "Abraham believed God, and...he was called the friend of God" (Jas. 2:23).
  2. The Lord knew Abraham personally (v. 19).
  3. The Lord revealed His plan to Abraham (v. 20-21).
  4. Abraham "still stood before the Lord" before responding to what the Lord had told him (v. 22).

B. **Solitude and Service Are Equally Essential.** Busy times of service must be balanced by quiet times of solitude with God.
  1. Solitude and service complement each other.
     a. Serving requires action; solitude involves waiting (v. 22).
     b. Serving is ministering to God; solitude is communing with Him.
     c. Often serving involves interaction with others; in solitude we interact with God alone.
  2. The Bible commands both solitude with God and service of God.
     a. Jesus will commend the Ephesian church for their work, but rebuke them for not spending time with Him: "I know your works...and you have persevered and have patience, and have labored for My name's sake and have not become weary. Nevertheless I have this against you, that you have left your first love" (Rev. 2:2-4).

b. Jesus commended Mary, "who also sat at Jesus' feet and heard His word," and rebuked Martha, who "was distracted with much serving...worried and troubled about many things" (Luke 10:38-42).

3. Solitude strengthens us for service.
   a. "For thus says the Lord God, the Holy One of Israel: 'In returning and rest you shall be saved; in *quietness* and *confidence* shall be your strength'" (Isa. 30:15).
   b. "Those who wait on the Lord shall *renew* their *strength*; they shall mount up with wings like eagles, they shall run and not be weary, they shall walk and not faint" (Isa. 40:31).

When a phone booth's door is closed, the light inside comes on and outside noise is shut out. Likewise, we need to shut the door on our world, get alone with God, and let Him reveal Himself to us.

III. Worship Involves Sacrifice (Genesis 22).

A. Abraham Obeyed and Trusted God. Throughout the greatest test of his faith, Abraham remained focused on God's resources rather than questioning His reasons.

1. "God tested Abraham" (v. 1).
2. Abraham answered when God called: "Here I am" (v. 1).
3. God told Abraham to: "Take now your son, your only son Isaac, whom you love, and go to the land of Moriah, and offer him there as a burnt offering..." (v. 2).

4. Abraham obeyed God's command: "Abraham rose early...and took...Isaac his son...and went to the place of which God had told him" (v. 3).
5. Abraham spoke of this painful sacrifice as an act of worship: "The lad and I will go yonder and worship" (v. 5).
   a. Paul also considered sacrifice a worship opportunity: "I...count all things loss for the excellence of the knowledge of Christ Jesus my Lord, for whom I have suffered the loss of all things...that I may know Him and the power of His resurrection, and the fellowship of His sufferings" (Phil. 3:8, 10).
   b. As He did with His disciples, Jesus sometimes uses the thing we fear most to come to us (Matt. 14:25-27; Mark 6:48-50).
6. Abraham had faith in God's promise and power. He told his men, "and *we* will come back to you" (v. 5, italics added).
   a. Abraham knew God had promised that his son would be his heir and his descendants would be as countless as the stars (Gen. 15:4-5; Heb. 11:17-19).
   b. Abraham believed God "was able to raise [Isaac] up, even from the dead" (Heb. 11:19).
   c. Perhaps Abraham remembered God's words to Sarah: "Is anything too hard for the LORD?" (Gen. 18:14).
7. Abraham learned to focus on the resources of God more than the reason why.

B. Service and Solitude Prepare the Way for Sacrifice.

1. Abraham's life of servitude to the Lord prepared him to obey God's command.
2. Abraham's friendship with the Lord prepared him to trust God.

C. **Sacrifice Should Be Continuous.** Worship through sacrifice is a way of life, a continuous demonstration to God of our love for Him.
   1. We sacrifice by surrendering. "Present your bodies a living sacrifice, holy, acceptable to God, which is your reasonable service" (Rom. 12:1).
   2. We sacrifice by praising. "By Him let us continually offer the sacrifice of praise to God, that is, the fruit of our lips, giving thanks to His name" (Heb. 13:15).
      a. No matter how we feel or what's going on in our lives, God remains worthy of our praise.
      b. Many great psalms and hymns have been written in times of struggle and pain.
   3. We sacrifice by giving.
      a. "But do not forget to do good and to share, for with such sacrifices God is well pleased" (Heb. 13:16).
      b. Paul tells the Philippians their gifts were "a sweet-smelling aroma, an acceptable sacrifice, well pleasing to God" (Phil. 4:18).
   4. We sacrifice by repenting.
      a. "For You do not desire sacrifice, or else I would give it; You do not delight in burnt offering. The sacrifices of God are a broken spirit, a broken and a contrite heart—these, O God, You will not despise (Ps. 51:16-17).
      b. Is your heart broken over your sins and failures? God will receive it as a sacrifice.

Father, we worship You by serving You. We worship You by being alone with You and regaining our strength in quietness. We worship You even through suffering, fear, grief, and sacrifice. We worship all You are, with all we are, because You are worthy.

1. What stage are you in with God—the receiving stage or the giving stage? How do you keep both in balance?

2. In what ways does God reveal His plan to you? How do you respond? How much alone time do you and God enjoy together during which He has your full attention?

3. During episodes of pain how do you respond to others? How do you respond to God? How could worship change things?

When God Let Down the Ladder

Genesis 28:10-22

According to The Gallup Organization, America's favorite hymn is *Amazing Grace.* Yet, a particular phrase in that song makes many of us wince: "saved a wretch like me." That's not America's favorite concept.

We are fallen and separated from God. Grace is God's attitude toward humanity. Grace is different from justice—getting what is deserved. It is not the same as mercy—not getting what we deserve. Grace is getting what is not deserved.

Jacob was a wretch when God found him. He was a fugitive running away from the trouble he had created. He was a manipulative liar and thief, seeking only his own advancement. Yet, God ran after him, showing him that what he thought was a dead-end street was actually a new beginning.

In Jacob's story, we see God lavishing His grace on an undeserving creature. In appropriate response, the creature (Jacob) worshiped the One who stooped to show such love.

I. The Dream: God Broke Through (v. 10-15).

After deceiving his father, Jacob's brother threatened to kill him (Gen. 27). To protect Jacob, his mother sent him to her brother in Haran, five hundred miles away. At the time of his dream, Jacob was somewhere between Beersheba and Haran.

A. What He Saw.

1. God sent the dream to get Jacob's attention. At this time Jacob was self-focused, discon-

nected from a relationship with God. God was determined to communicate with Jacob.

2. When God speaks in a dream, it says something about the person's attitude toward God.
   a. God doesn't often speak in dreams.
   b. God first tries to speak through His Word and the Holy Spirit.
   c. God used other ways to reach Jonah, Peter, and Saul (Jonah 1:1-2; Acts 9:3-6, 10:9-15, 16:9, 18:9).
3. Jacob saw God reaching down to him from heaven.
4. Jacob saw a ladder leading from heaven to earth (v. 12). This could be translated as a staircase or a ramp.
5. Jacob saw "angels of God...ascending and descending on" the ladder (v. 12).
   a. The angels ascending had been previously on earth.
   b. The angels descending were coming to earth to serve.
6. Jacob saw God standing above the ladder (v. 13).
7. All this symbolizes God's sovereign control and presence over both heaven and earth.
   a. We can't reach God (or heaven) through our own efforts to create religion (i.e. the tower of Babel, Gen. 11:1-9).
   b. Only God can bridge the gap between heaven and earth, between us and Him—through relationship.

B. **What He Heard** (Gen. 28:13-15). Jacob heard the voice of God blessing him with three promises.
   1. Promise of provision. "The land on which you lie I will give to you" (v. 13).

   a. This is the same promise God made to Jacob's grandfather, Abraham, and father, Isaac: the Abrahamic covenant.
   b. Jacob had just stolen his brother's blessing from their father, yet God blessed him further.
2. Promise of presence. "I am with you" (v. 15).
3. Promise of protection. "I will keep you wherever you go, and will bring you back to this land; for I will not leave you until I have done what I have spoken to you" (v. 15).
4. Jacob's behavior deserved punishment, but God blessed him instead. His life was headed for delinquency, but God intervened with grace.
   a. God intervened and spoke to Jacob because of who He is; not because of who Jacob was.
   b. Grace is God acting according to His own nature. We can never earn it.
   c. No matter how badly we have acted in the past, and no matter how ashamed we are of it, God is able to meet us where we are and make us a channel of blessing.

If you need a cleaner soul, Jesus can do the job. If you are searching for Him, stand still, and He will find you. If you are afraid of being a hypocrite, the most authentic thing you can do is trust Him with your life. You can have a new start with Him today.

II. The Discovery: God Is Here (v. 16-17).

Through the dream, Jacob discovered God's presence and his own ignorance.

A. **"Surely the Lord Is in This Place"** (v. 16). In an unexpected place, Jacob discovered God's omnipresence.
   1. Jacob used the present tense: "*is* in this place" (italics added), meaning God was, is, and always will be there.
   2. David, too, discovered and described God's presence: "O Lord, you have examined my heart and know everything about me. You know when I sit down or stand up. You know my every thought when far away. You chart the path ahead of me and tell me where to stop and rest. Every moment you know where I am...You both precede and follow me...I can never escape from your spirit! I can never get away from your presence" (Ps. 139:1-7, TLB).
      a. Overwhelmed, David's response was worship: "Such knowledge is too wonderful for me; it is high, I cannot attain it" (Ps. 139:6).
   3. Thomas discovered God's omnipresence (John 20:24-29).
      a. Thomas had expressed his doubts about Jesus' resurrection to the other disciples: "Unless I see in His hands the print of the nails, and put my finger into the print of the nails, and put my hand into His side, I will not believe" (John 20:25).
      b. When Jesus saw Thomas, with gentle grace He indicated His knowledge of Thomas' doubts: "Reach your finger here, and look at My hands; and reach your hand here, and put it into My side" (John 20:27).
      c. Thomas responded with worship: "My Lord and my God!" (John 20:28).

B. **"And I Did Not Know It"** (v. 16). Jacob admitted his unawareness.

1. Like Jacob, David, and Thomas, many of us struggle with grasping and living lives that reflect the truth of God's omnipresence.
2. God is never more than a ladder away—and He reminds us when we forget.

III. The Decision: God Shall Be My God (v. 18-22).

Jacob's discovery of God's omnipresence led him to respond in three different ways.

A. He Worshiped by Commemorating (v. 18-19). Jacob worshiped God by building a memorial of his encounter there with God.

1. He created a pillar using the stone he had put at his head the night before, marking it with oil (v. 18).
2. He renamed the place (originally called Luz) Bethel, which means "God's house" (v. 19).
   a. Two generations earlier, Abraham had built an altar to the Lord on a "mountain east of Bethel...with Bethel on the west and Ai on the east" (Gen. 12:8).
   b. The simplicity of the memorial and the name Jacob chose symbolize his recognition that God is everywhere—that any place can be God's house.

KEY THOUGHT

God's revelation demands man's resolution. When God lets down His ladder to reveal Himself in a place where you think He's not present, commemorate that place to Him and commit your whole life to Him in worship.

B. He Worshiped by Committing (v. 20-22). Jacob worshiped God by vowing to devote his life to Him.

1. He accepted God's promise to him: "If God will be with me, and keep me in this way that I am going, and give me bread to eat and clothing to put on, so that I come back to my father's house in peace..." (v. 20-21).
    a. By beginning his sentence with "if," Jacob was not bargaining with God. He was simply restating what God had promised during the night.
    b. Many scholars say "since" or "because" better reflect the intent of Jacob's statement.
2. He responded to God's promises with his own: "...then the LORD shall be my God...and of all that You give me I will surely give a tenth to You" (v. 21-22).

C. **He Worshiped by Contributing.** Jacob worshiped God by promising a tenth of his income to God.
1. Jacob's contribution was voluntary. It predated the law given to Moses that required Israel to give a tenth to the Lord.
2. Jacob's contribution indicated a changed heart: "For where your treasure is, there your heart will be also" (Luke 12:34).
3. Jacob worshiped God by keeping his vow. His life was not perfect from this point forward, yet Scripture shows this was a turning point in his life.

As flawed and manipulative as Jacob was, God let the ladder down and gave him a new beginning. It is important to note that God let the ladder down—man did not build it up to God. Each of us is unworthy and unable to connect with God on our own. Yet, because grace is God's nature, He provided us with a ladder to Him: Jesus, His Son (John 14:6). All we have to do is hear and accept His truth, and respond to Him in worship with our lives.

1. Has God ever broken into your busy life to bless you in a way that was totally unexpected? What did you learn from it? How did you respond?
2. In what ways do you commemorate God's work in your life and relationship with you?
3. Is worship becoming a part of your lifestyle or is it merely episodic?

Bowing Before the Battle Begins

Joshua 5:13–6:6

Following God's plan for our lives is the most rewarding, exciting, and challenging way to live. It's an adventure! It's also a full-time, high-stakes war. God's army is guaranteed victory, but the battle must first be fought to completion.

Before we became Christians, we were hostages in Satan's camp—separated from God. Then God rescued us, using His Word and His soldiers, and His Son to show us the way out of captivity. Once freed, we became soldiers in God's army, fighting to rescue other hostages and striving to become better soldiers.

Inarguably, the battle is well worth fighting for our Commander. Yet, it also takes a toll. Many of God's soldiers become beat up and burned out on the battlefield. How can we stay strong and alert amidst adversity and conflict? The answer may surprise you—a life of worship! Joshua shows us how.

I. The Plan of God: Canaan (v. 10-12).

- **A. A Leader Appointed.** Just as God appointed Moses to lead Israel out of Egypt, He appointed Joshua to lead Israel into Canaan.
  1. God appointed Joshua to lead Israel into the Promised Land (Num. 27:18-21; Deut. 1:38, 31:23).
  2. God promised Joshua success: "Your eyes have seen all that the LORD your God has done to these two kings; so will the LORD do to all the kingdoms through which you pass. You must

not fear them, for the LORD your God Himself fights for you" (Deut. 3:21b-22).

3. God blessed Joshua with wisdom: "Now Joshua the son of Nun was full of the spirit of wisdom, for Moses had laid his hands on him..." (Deut. 34:9).
4. God promised Joshua His presence: "This day I will begin to exalt you in the sight of all Israel, that they may know that, as I was with Moses, so I will be with you" (Josh. 3:7).

B. **A Promise Kept.** By bringing Israel to Canaan, God kept the promise He made through Moses.
   1. The desert and wilderness were not God's ultimate goal for His people.
   2. God delivered Israel from Egypt to deliver them to Canaan.

C. **A Representation of Things to Come.** Canaan symbolically represents God's plan for mankind—not just Israel.
   1. Some have compared Canaan to heaven, and crossing the Jordan to death.
      a. If this parallel were accurate, it would mean we will have to fight in heaven. The Israelites' occupation of Canaan was punctuated by battles.
      b. In contrast, the Bible tells us about heaven: "And God will wipe away every tear from their eyes; there shall be no more death, nor sorrow, nor crying. There shall be no more pain, for the former things have passed away" (Rev. 21:4).
   2. For the Christian, Canaan represents God's desire for each Christian's life: abundance, blessing, His presence, His path, and the fulfillment of His promises.

D. **Enjoying Canaan: A Process.** Canaan was a gift from God; Israel did not earn it.
  1. It was a gift they inherited as a process.
    a. They had to walk: "Every place that the sole of your foot will tread upon I have given you..." (Josh. 1:3).
    b. They had to fight the battles to claim the gift: "I will not drive them out from before you in one year, lest the land become desolate and the beasts of the field become too numerous for you. Little by little I will drive them out from before you, until you have increased, and you inherit the land" (Ex. 23:29-30).
  2. The process made them dependent on God.
  3. Like Canaan, our Christianity is a gift we did not earn.
    a. We must walk: "If we live in the Spirit, let us also walk in the Spirit" (Gal. 5:25).
    b. We must fight: "Put on the whole armor of God, that you may be able to stand against the wiles of the devil ..." (Eph. 6:11).

E. **Canaan: Never Totally Possessed** (Josh. 1:4). Canaan was a larger gift than Israel wanted or used.
  1. They did not claim all that God wanted to give them.
    a. Canaan was three hundred thousand square miles.
    b. Israel never occupied more than one-tenth of that.
  2. Our Christianity is an extravagant gift.
    a. Our borders of spiritual influence are vast.
    b. Too often, we are content to live with one small part of what God has promised, rather than exploring the abundance with which God has blessed us.

II. The Predicament of God's People: Jericho.

A. **A History of Fear.** Israel's forefathers had forfeited Canaan because of fear.

1. Forty years earlier, Moses had dispatched a spy delegation into Canaan.
2. The spies' report was pessimistic: "We are not able to go up against the people, for they are stronger than we...The land...devours its inhabitants, and all the people whom we saw in it are men of great stature" (Num. 13:31-32).
   a. Only Joshua and Caleb delivered a positive report: "Let us go up at once and take possession, for we are well able to overcome it...If the LORD delights in us, then He will bring us into this land and give it to us...Only do not rebel against the LORD, nor fear the people of the land, for...their protection has departed from them, and the LORD is with us. Do not fear them" (Num. 13:30, 14:8-9).
   b. Of the Israelites living at that time, only Joshua and Caleb entered the Promised Land (Num. 14:30, 38).
3. Responding in fear, Israel "would not go up, but rebelled against the command of the LORD" (Deut. 1:26).

B. **An Uneven Battle.** To the human eye, Israel's victory seemed impossible.

1. Jericho had high, thick walls: "The cities are great and fortified up to heaven..." (Deut. 1:28). The children of Israel were on foot.
2. Jericho was well armed; the Israelites had rocks, arrows, and spears.
3. Jericho's army was comprised of professional fighters; the Israelites were ex-slaves and wilderness travelers.

4. Jericho was protected; Israel was exposed: "Now Jericho was securely shut up because of the children of Israel; none went out, and none came in" (Josh. 6:1).

C. **A Scene Set by God.** Because Canaan was God's plan, Jericho was also part of God's plan.

1. "Jerichos" in our lives—seemingly insurmountable obstacles—are part of God's plan for each of us.
2. They indicate that we're on the right path: "Because narrow is the gate and difficult is the way which leads to life, and there are few who find it" (Matt. 7:14).
3. They remind us we can do nothing apart from God: "The things which are impossible with men are possible with God" (Luke 18:27).

KEY THOUGHT

Many Christians drop out of the war because they don't pause to worship between battles. Public victories are the result of private visits.

III. The Prerequisite for God's Power: An Encounter (Josh. 5:13-15). Before we can do battle for God, we must worship Him.

A. **Identify the Commander.** The Man who appeared to Joshua identified himself as "Commander of the army of the LORD" (v. 14).

1. The Events: Abraham worshiped.
   a. A Man appeared in front of Joshua "with His sword drawn in His hand" (v. 13).
   b. Joshua requested identification: "Are You for us or for our adversaries?" (v. 13).

c. The Man responded: "No, but as Commander of the army of the LORD I have now come" (v. 14).
d. Joshua immediately responded in worship: "Joshua fell on his face to the earth and worshiped, and said to Him, 'What does my Lord say to His servant?'" (v. 14).

2. The Commander: Jesus Christ.
   a. He was not an angel; angels do not allow themselves to be worshiped (Rev. 19:10; 22:8-9).
   b. He was not a prophet or a man called to serve God; men of God refuse worship (Acts 14:11-18).
   c. He was not God the Father.
      i. God the Father refused to let Himself be seen. When Moses asked to see God's face, He responded: "You cannot see My face; for no man shall see Me, and live" (Ex. 33:20).
      ii. In the New Testament, we read, "No one has seen God at any time. The only begotten Son, who is in the bosom of the Father, He has declared Him" (John 1:18).
   d. He was Jesus Christ in pre-incarnate form.
      i. Jacob wrestled with God in this form: "For I have seen God face to face, and my life is preserved" (Gen. 32:30).
      ii. In this form, God spoke with Moses: "So the LORD spoke to Moses face to face, as a man speaks to his friend" (Ex. 33:11).
      iii. Of Himself, Jesus said, "He who has seen Me has seen the Father..." (John 14:9).

iv. Paul wrote, "[Christ] is the image of the invisible God, the firstborn over all creation" (Col. 1:15).

v. The writer of Hebrews wrote, "The Son is the radiance of God's glory and the exact representation of His being..." (Heb. 1:3, NIV).

B. **Align Yourself with the Commander.** Joshua aligned himself by recognizing the Commander's authority.

1. Wrong Question: "Are You for us or for our adversaries?" (v. 13).
   a. By asking the Commander this question, Joshua indicated the fact that he thought he was in charge.
2. Right Answer: "No, but as Commander of the army of the Lord I have now come" (v. 14).
   a. The Commander's response corrected Joshua, letting him know that he, not Joshua, was in charge.
   b. The Commander was the Commander of all the armies of heaven—not just Israel's army.
      i. This explains the crumbling of Jericho's walls in response to Israel's mere marching, shouting, and blowing of trumpets (Josh. 6:1-20).
      ii. When the enemy surrounded Israel's army, and Elisha's servant panicked, Elisha prayed: "'LORD, I pray, open his eyes that he may see'...And behold, the mountain was full of horses and chariots of fire all around Elisha" (2 Kings 6:17).
      iii. Jesus referred to the Lord's army during His arrest in the Garden of Gethsemane: "Do you think that I

cannot now pray to My Father, and He will provide Me with more than twelve legions of angels?" (Matt. 26:53).

3. Right Response: "What does my Lord say to His servant?" (v. 14).
    a. We should ask God what He wants us to do rather than telling Him what we want Him to do.
    b. When it seems as if our plans have gone awry, we should pray in worship: "Lord, You are God, who made heaven and earth and the sea, and all that is in them" (Acts 4:24).

C. **Worship the Commander.**
1. Worship by adoration. Joshua humbled himself in obedience and submission.
    a. In response to the Commander's command, Joshua took off his sandals (v. 15).
        i. This is a sign of submission to authority.
        ii. It is also a demonstration of trust; in doing so, Joshua placed himself at risk of being caught unprepared.
    b. He "fell on his face to the earth and worshiped" (v. 14).
    c. Adoring worship toward God is a powerful weapon against Satan.
2. Worship by meditation. God had previously instructed Joshua to meditate (Josh. 1:8).
    a. Meditation is a component of achieving God's goals: "For then you will make your way prosperous, and then you will have good success" (Josh. 1:8).
    b. God's Word reveals strategy, outcomes, and information about both our Commander and our enemy.

c. Meditation integrates these truths into our minds, hearts, and lives—making them more available whenever we need them.

3. Worship by action. Joshua worshiped through obedience of the Lord's command.
   a. The Lord promised His power: "See! I have given Jericho into your hand, its king, and the mighty men of valor" (Josh. 6:2).
   b. Joshua obeyed the Lord's command to "march around the city, all you men of war; you shall go all around the city once" (Josh. 6:3).
      i. Adoration and meditation should lead to action.
      ii. Obedience is the ultimate expression of worship; without obedience, there is no worship.
      iii. Jesus said, "If you love Me, keep My commandments" (John 14:15).

Battles are inevitable. They're a normal part of the life of a believer. To fight each battle we encounter successfully, we must remember who is in charge. We should check in with Him often, to learn more of His battle plan, and respond to Him with adoration, meditation, and obedience.

1. What "battles" have you faced in your life? How has your relationship with Christ made a difference in the way you handled them? What role did worship play in these battles?

2. In what ways do people try to put God on their side, and then pit themselves against others? What greater issue is at stake?

3. How will you move your worship from a weekly experience at church to a daily experience on the battlefield?

Worship from an Ash Heap
Job 1:6-22

Worship is easy when life is good—when the cupboards are full, when we and our loved ones are healthy, when the sun shines and we have time to enjoy it. But songs sung during the dark nights of affliction and loss can only come from God.

You've probably experienced suffering. If you haven't yet, you will. Suffering shakes our faith and causes us to ask questions we perhaps thought we'd never ask. "God, if you're such a good God, why can such things happen?" I've asked those questions. My life was shaken when my brother was killed in a motorcycle accident; when my father died; and when my wife and I lost a baby just three months into the pregnancy.

Job had the worst possible day in anyone's life. He literally lost more than most of us will ever have to lose. Yet his response to suffering compels us to move to a deeper level of worship—the worship of a broken heart.

I. An Unseen Supernatural Reality (v. 6-12).

God and Satan discussed Job's life, character, and welfare. Scripture labels Job as "blameless and upright, and one who feared God and shunned evil" (v. 1). He had a large family, was prosperous, and influential. Of all people, Job did not "deserve" to suffer. This invalidates the argument that Christians should not suffer—that suffering is a result of sin.

A. Satan Is Real. Scripture tells us of Satan's existence, intent, and activities.

1. Paul wrote to the Ephesians: "For we do not wrestle against flesh and blood, but against principalities, against powers, against the rulers of the darkness of this age, against spiritual hosts of wickedness in the heavenly places" (Eph. 6:12).
2. Daniel was visited by an angel who had been detained by "the prince of the kingdom of Persia." The angel delivered the message, then returned to continue fighting the spiritual battle (Dan. 10:13, 20).

B. **Satan Is Active.** Satan described his activities to God as "going to and fro on the earth, and from walking back and forth on it" (v. 7).
   1. He recruits for his own kingdom (Mark 4:15).
   2. He persecutes and tempts God's children (Mark 8:33; Acts 5:3; 2 Cor. 2:11).
   3. He studies people.
      a. He studied Job.
      b. He studied Peter (Luke 22:31).

C. **God Has Power Over Satan and His Loving Eye Is on Us.**
   1. Satan may only act with permission from God.
      a. Satan asked for and received permission to persecute Job (v. 11-12).
      b. Jesus told Peter, "Satan has asked for you, that he may sift you as wheat" (Luke 22:31).
      c. When being cast out of a man by Jesus, "the demons begged Him" to be allowed to enter a herd of swine. Jesus granted their request (Matt. 8:31-32).
   2. God protects us: "God is faithful, who will not allow you to be tempted beyond what you are able, but with the temptation will also make the way of escape, that you may be able to bear it" (1 Cor. 10:13).

a. Satan challenged the validity of Job's worship of God.
b. God met Satan's challenge, knowing He would win: "Behold, all that he has is in your power" (v. 12).
c. God set parameters to limit Satan's power: "...only do not lay a hand on his person" (v. 12).

II. An Unthinkable Natural Calamity (v. 13-19).

With God's permission, Satan struck Job's life with tragedy.

A. Job Lost All He Owned Except Four Servants.

Sons, daughters, servants, livestock, and real estate were all destroyed at once.

1. Job was a man endorsed by God's Word as "blameless and upright" (v. 1), yet he suffered from unthinkable loss.
2. This raises the issue of theodicy, which is "vindication of God's goodness and justice in the face of the existence of evil" (Merriam-Webster's Collegiate Dictionary).
   a. This is disturbing to all of us, especially if this is what happened to the most godly man on earth at that time.
   b. There is no guarantee that Jesus will take all the bad and difficult events from our lives.
   c. Though protected by God, we are all vulnerable to suffering.

B. Job Only Knew Half the Story.

1. Job did not know about the supernatural conversation about him between Satan and God. He knew what had happened to him, but he did not know why.
2. We have the advantage of going backstage to see why everything happened to Job.

III. An Uncanny Spiritual Activity (v. 20-22).
Job grieved...then worshiped!

A. The Expected Demonstration of Grief (v. 20). Job responded to his tragedy humanly. He wasn't a stoically spiritual person with no emotion.

1. Job expressed his grief profoundly.
2. Job expressed his grief culturally: He "tore his robe, and shaved his head" (v. 20).
3. Job expressed his grief naturally, appropriately, and healthily.
4. Natural grief usually includes several stages, including denial, anger, depression, bargaining, and acceptance.

B. The Unexpected Demonstration of Worship (v. 20-22). Job responded to his tragedy with spiritual maturity.

1. Job "fell to the ground and worshiped. And he said: ...Blessed be the name of the Lord" (v. 20-21).
2. This act demonstrates Job's true character. Times of grief and suffering reveal the strength of our faith.

C. Three Principles (v. 21-22). Job's response teaches us how to respond to God in challenging circumstances.

1. Our grasp on life must be light because our lives are not ours.
   a. Job said: "Naked I came from my mother's womb, and naked shall I return there" (v. 21).
   b. The apostle Paul later wrote: "For we brought nothing into this world, and it is certain we can carry nothing out" (1 Tim. 6:7).
2. Our God must be enthroned: He is sovereign.

a. Job recognized God's sovereignty and power: "The LORD gave, and the LORD has taken away; blessed be the name of the LORD" (v. 21).
b. Job recognized the things that he had been given as a gift from God. There was nothing that he had earned or deserved.
c. Both blessing and suffering are part of God's perfect plan for us (1 Pet. 2:20; 3:17).

3. Our goal must be submission.
   a. Job submitted to God in worship: "In all of this, Job did not sin by blaming God" (v. 22, NLT).
   b. Job maintained his submission, even under criticism: "Though He slay me, yet will I trust Him" (Job. 13:15).
   c. The way to address adversity is by keeping our eyes on the Lord rather than on our circumstances.

MAKE THE CONNECTION

Many of us have endured and are still enduring periods of deep pain, loss, and grief. God, in His wisdom, has included in His Word the true story of Job, a man who endured total loss of family, assets, position, comfort, friendship, physical health, and his wife's loyalty. Yet, despite the circumstances, he worshiped his Lord. Like Job, we can prepare for and endure suffering by holding our own lives lightly, enthroning God through a lifestyle of worship, and faithfully and humbly submitting to His sovereign plan for our lives.

1. What are some characteristics about your personality you think Satan has taken note of and may try to exploit for his purposes (i.e., habits, weaknesses, patterns)?

2. If you were in Job's place as the subject being discussed between Satan and God, would Satan be right in thinking you worship God only when everything is going your way and God is blessing you?
3. What rights does God have over your life? Your possessions? Your family and friends? How do you respond to Him when He adds or removes them?

A Worship That Transforms

Isaiah 6:1-8

If worship doesn't change us, it hasn't been true worship. None of us can stand, kneel, or bow in genuine worship before the Holy One of eternity and remain unchanged. As we've seen time after time in the previous chapters, encounters with God dramatically transformed lives.

We'll see this again in the life of Isaiah, a prophet who saw and heard something so unique it changed him for good. Isaiah experienced the permanent change of a life lived for God.

I. What He Saw: Vision (v. 1-2).

- **A. Isaiah Saw God on a Throne in a Temple.**
  1. The vision occurred in 739 BC, the year King Uzziah died and the enemy was threatening Israel.
     - a. King Uzziah had ruled for fifty-two years with positive influence. He was godly and prosperous.
     - b. Since King Uzziah's death, the Assyrian Empire had taken over Northern Israel and was threatening Jerusalem.
     - c. The Israelites were grieving the loss of their king and filled with fear for themselves.
       - i. Perhaps the Israelites felt as the psalmist who wrote, "If the foundations are destroyed, what can the righteous do?" (Ps. 11:3)

ii. Recent surveys say our society today, like the Israelites, views the future with apprehension.

2. The vision reminded Isaiah that God was still on His throne, even though King Uzziah was no longer on his.

B. **God Is on His Throne Today.** No matter what happens in life, the heavenly throne is secure. The world skews our vision. If we become caught up in the events surrounding us, we will forget that God is still on His throne.

1. If we allow the world to skew our vision, we will begin limiting God by our human perspective.
   a. The children of Israel "limited the Holy One of Israel. They did not remember His power..." (Ps. 78:41b-42).
   b. Jesus was limited by the unbelief of the people in His hometown: "He did not do many mighty works there because of their unbelief" (Matt. 13:58).
2. Worship realigns our vision.
   a. Like a telescope, worship brings God close and into focus, showing us that He is far bigger than our problems.
   b. Worship reminds us that God is unlimited, all-powerful, and still on the throne.
      i. We need to be reminded to worship. Asaph wrote about this, saying, "But as for me, my feet had almost stumbled; my steps had nearly slipped. For I was envious of the boastful, when I saw the prosperity of the wicked... Until I went into the sanctuary of God; then I understood their end" (Ps. 73:2-3, 17).

Worship reminds us that God never panics.
—Oswald Chambers

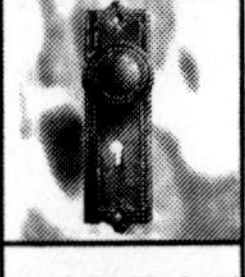

KEY THOUGHT

C. **Isaiah Saw Seraphim.** Seraphim—angelic beings—stood above the throne.
   1. *Seraph* means "blazing one, zealous one, burning one."
   2. The seraphim seem to be guardians of the blazing glory and holiness of God.
   3. Each seraph had six wings.
      a. Two wings covered the face, indicating that they dare not gaze on the glory of God.
      b. Two wings covered the feet, indicating humility before God.
      c. Two wings allowed the seraph to fly, doing God's bidding.
      d. Of the six wings, four serve the purpose of worship; two facilitate service.
         i. Worship, being paramount, comes first.
         ii. Service comes out of worship.

II. **What He Heard: Voices** (v. 3-4).

A. **The Seraphim Worshiped.** "One cried to another" (v. 3).
   1. They worshiped loudly: "And the posts of the door were shaken by the voice of him who cried out" (v. 4).
   2. They worshiped God's holiness: "Holy, holy, holy is the LORD of hosts" (v. 3).
      a. "Holy, holy, holy" is called the trihagion.
      b. The trihagion emphasizes the essential character of God: His holiness.

c. *Holy* means "sacred, saint, set apart" (Brown, Driver, Briggs, Gesenius Lexicon).

B. God's Holiness Is an Essential Part of Worship.

1. Worship is about God's holiness, not our happiness.
2. Through our lifestyle of worship, God wants to make us holy.
3. Holiness facilitates happiness.
   a. God's essential character is holiness.
   b. God's character is also joy and love.

C. The Dramatic Effect on Isaiah. When Isaiah saw God in all of His holiness, he saw himself as he was in his sinfulness. When seen next to the purity of God, the impurity of man is all the more evident. Worship expresses the idea that: God is awesome, I am undeserving of Him.

1. As a prophet, Isaiah's God-given calling was to recognize and point out sin.
   a. "Woe to those who join house to house; they add field to field, till there is no place where they may dwell alone in the midst of the land" (Isa. 5:8).
   b. "Woe to those who rise early in the morning, that they may follow intoxicating drink; who continue until night, till wine inflames them" (Isa. 5:11).
   c. "Woe to those who draw iniquity with cords of vanity, and sin as if with a cart rope" (Isa. 5:18).
   d. "Woe to those who call evil good, and good evil; who put darkness for light, and light for darkness; who put bitter for sweet, and sweet for bitter! Woe to those who are wise in their own eyes, and prudent in their own sight! Woe to men mighty at drinking wine, woe to men

valiant for mixing intoxicating drink, who justify the wicked for a bribe, and take away justice from the righteous man" (Isa. 5:20-23).

2. In God's presence, Isaiah had a true worship experience.
   a. He saw God for who God is: "the King, the LORD of hosts" (v. 5).
   b. He saw himself for who he was: "Woe is me, for I am undone! Because I am a man of unclean lips, and I dwell in the midst of a people of unclean lips; for my eyes have seen the King, the LORD of hosts" (v. 5).
   c. True worship reminds us of who God is: awesome, holy, separate from us; and who we are: undeserving and unworthy of Him.
      i. Paul experienced true worship: "This is a faithful saying and worthy of all acceptance, that Christ Jesus came into the world to save sinners, of whom I am chief" (1 Tim. 1:15).
      ii. Job experienced true worship: "I have heard of You by the hearing of the ear, but now my eye sees You. Therefore I abhor myself, and repent in dust and ashes" (Job 42:5-6).
      iii. Peter experienced true worship: "When Simon Peter saw it, he fell down at Jesus' knees, saying, 'Depart from me, for I am a sinful man, O Lord!'" (Luke 5:8).

III. What He Felt: Victory (v. 6-8).

Isaiah was purified of his sin: "Then one of the seraphim flew to me, having in his hand a live coal which he had taken with the tongs from the altar. And he touched my mouth with it, and said: 'Behold, this has touched your lips; your iniquity is taken away, and your sin purged'" (v. 6-7).

A. **Isaiah Had Confessed His Sin—Unclean Lips.** The coal purified his lips.
B. **Jewish Law Required Purification Before Worship.** The seraphim purified Isaiah, enabling him to worship.
C. **Worship Reminds Us of Who We Are.** Worship reminds us of what we've done, and why we need God's forgiveness.
D. **Worship Should Fill Us With Joy.** We have joy because of God's forgiveness, rather than woe because of our sinfulness.

IV. What He Did: Volunteer (v. 8-9a).

True worship involves action.

A. **True Worship is Active.**
   1. Isaiah's experience of conviction and purification wouldn't have led to worship if it was not followed by his response: "Then I said, 'Here am I! Send me'" (v. 8).
   2. Isaiah's encounter with God transformed his life, filling him with the desire to serve.
   3. The active ministry we perform reflects the influence of true worship in our lives.

B. **Worship and Service Go Together.**
   1. In the New King James Version, there are twenty-nine verses that contain both "worship" and "serve."
   2. Some Scriptures translate these terms appositionally; one means the other.
   3. Worship leads to service.
      a. Our first cry to God must be, "Here I am, Lord. Save me." (Luke 19:10)

   b. Our second cry to God must be, "Here I am, Lord. Sanctify me." (1 Thess. 5:23)
   c. Our third cry to God must be, "Here am I Lord. Send me." (Isa. 6:8)

C. True Worship Is Voluntary.

1. God asked Isaiah, "Whom shall I send, and who will go for Us?" (Isa. 6:8).
2. God uses human volunteers to reach other human hearts.
3. God will use anyone willing to be used by Him.
   a. God doesn't call just the qualified; He qualifies those He calls.
   b. God can accomplish more through weakness than strength, more through humility than pride, more through simplicity than complexity.
      i. God created man out of common dust (Gen. 2:7).
      ii. God spoke to Moses through a burning bush in the middle of a desert (Ex. 3:2-4).
      iii. Jesus was raised in Nazareth: "Can anything good come out of Nazareth?" (John 1:46).
      iv. After crossing the Jordan, Joshua built a memorial to the Lord using common river stones (Josh. 4:8-9).
      v. David killed Goliath using a simple sling and stone (1 Sam. 17:49-50).

Before He returned to heaven from earth, Jesus gave his disciples the Great Commission: "Go...and make disciples of all the nations" (Matt. 28:19). As disciples of Christ, those instructions are for us as well.

But we can't perform the Great Commission if there's a great omission in our lives: the omission of worship. Before we can influence others' lives for Christ, our own hearts and lives must first be transformed—through genuine worship.

1. How have you heard God speak to you in the past? Through reading the Bible or hearing a message in church? Was it by listening to a radio program or through the counsel of a thoughtful mature Christian friend? How appropriate was your response?
2. How much is the holiness of God a part of your personal worship? How does it affect you?
3. In what areas of ministry are you currently involved? When you see a need, is your response "Here I am Lord; send me"?

The Lavish Worship of an Overflowing Heart

John 12:1-8

For some Christians Sunday is a kind of "visiting day"—a day they go to God's house to visit Him a few hours each week. Is it for you? Do you stay in touch with God throughout the week—at work, the car wash, the grocery store, and your home?

What about when you're really grateful to God for something He's done? Do you express your gratitude? Or are you worried about how people would react if you appeared "too spiritual" or "too excited" about God?

Mary of Bethany is a refreshing, inspiring example of an adoring worshiper who lavished her love on Christ. She loved Jesus with the kind of love, and worshiped Him with the reckless worship that didn't care who was watching or what they were thinking.

I. Her Heart Was Grateful (v. 1-3).

During Passover week, Jesus, Mary, Martha, Lazarus, and the disciples were invited to dinner by Simon the leper. Simon was probably a leper that Jesus had healed. Jesus often stayed in Bethany when He came to Jerusalem and this stay was different—it was His final visit to Jerusalem.

- **A. Mary's Reason.** Mary's worship flowed out of her gratitude to Jesus and it was lavish. Jesus had raised Mary's brother from the dead.
    1. Lazarus, who was Mary and Martha's brother, had become sick (John 11:1-2).

2. The sisters sent word to Jesus (John 11:3).
3. Lazarus died (John 11:14).
4. Jesus had arrived on the fourth day after Lazarus' death (John 11:17).
5. Mary wept at Jesus' feet, crying, "Lord, if You had been here, my brother would not have died" (John 11:32).
6. Jesus restored Lazarus to life (John 11:43-44).

B. **Mary's Relationship with Jesus.** Mary frequently spent time at Jesus' feet.
   1. She poured oil on His feet (v. 3).
   2. She fell at Jesus' feet when she saw Him after her brother's death: "When Mary came where Jesus was, and saw Him, she fell down at His feet" (John 11:32).
   3. On another occasion, she sat at Jesus' feet to hear His word (Luke 10:39).

C. **Mary's Worship.** Mary worshiped at Jesus' feet.
   1. Many people came to Jesus' feet with needs: "Then great multitudes came to Him, having with them the lame, blind, mute, maimed, and many others; and they laid them down at Jesus' feet, and He healed them" (Matt. 15:30).
   2. Mary came to Jesus' feet this time with a gift, not a need.

D. **Martha's Worship.** Martha worshiped through serving.
   1. Previously, Martha had served without an attitude of worship: "But Martha was distracted with much serving, and she approached Him and said, 'Lord, do You not care that my sister has left me to serve alone? Therefore tell her to help me'" (Luke 10:40).
   2. This time, we simply read "and Martha served" (John 12:2).

3. Martha's service had become worship, perhaps out of gratitude to Jesus for restoring her brother's life.

Is your worship lavish, flowing out of a heart filled with gratitude, or is it routine, driven by habit, obligation, or appearance?

II. Her Gift Was Valuable (v. 3, 5).
Mary gave generously and sacrificially.

- **A. She Gave the Best.** Mary anointed Jesus with "a pound of very costly oil of spikenard" (v. 3).
  1. The oil was the best available.
     - a. Oil of spikenard was an exotic oil from a plant grown only in India.
     - b. It was usually found only in wealthy homes or at a feast, and was used sparingly.
     - c. Scripture tells us it was "very costly" (v. 3) and worth "three hundred denarii" (v. 5).
       - i. This amount is equal to almost a year's average wage.
       - ii. Conservative estimates place its value at $25,000–$30,000.
  2. The oil was in an alabaster flask that was also valuable (Mark 14:3).
     - a. Alabaster was a fine marble quarried in Egypt and delicately hand-crafted into small containers. It was very costly.
     - b. Because Mary was not a woman of means, the oil-filled flask may have been an heirloom.
- **B. She Gave It All.**
  1. She broke the flask; she did not save it to use for something else (Mark 14:3).
  2. She poured the entire amount out on Jesus.

C. **She Gave True Worship.** Mary's gift was given from the heart, placing Jesus above all else.
   1. True worship is the proper response to God from our hearts, whereby we place God above everyone and everything else.
      a. She placed God above herself by giving Him what was perhaps her most valuable possession.
      b. She placed God above herself by not caring how others would react.
   2. True worship is voluntarily sacrificial.
      a. Mary gave Jesus something that held high value for her.
      b. Similarly, David insisted on paying for a field he intended to use for God's temple because he refused to give anything to God that did not cost him anything (1 Chron. 21:18-26).

III. Her Critics Were Disagreeable (v. 4-8).

Mary was criticized by others whose vision was clouded by their own sin.

A. **The Criticism.** "Why was this fragrant oil not sold for three hundred denarii and given to the poor?" (v. 5).

B. **The Critics.**
   1. The first to criticize was Judas, "one of His disciples, Judas Iscariot, Simon's son, who would betray Him" (v. 4).
   2. The other disciples agreed: They were "indignant" and "criticized her sharply" (Matt. 26:8; Mark 14:4-5).

C. **The Motive.** "This he said, not that he cared for the poor, but because he was a thief, and had the money box; and he used to take what was put in it" (v. 6).

1. Judas criticized Mary based on the greed and guilt in his own heart.
   a. He accused Mary of stealing from the poor; yet he was stealing from the Lord.
   b. He criticized Mary about three hundred denarii; just days later he betrayed Jesus for a mere thirty pieces of silver.
2. Jesus talked about the human tendency to criticize others for our own faults: "And why do you look at the speck in your brother's eye, but do not consider the plank in your own eye?... Hypocrite! First remove the plank from your own eye, and then you will see clearly to remove the speck from your brother's eye" (Matt. 7:3, 5).
3. David also reacted strongly to being reminded of his own sin by someone else's life (2 Sam. 12:1-10).
   a. David prescribed death for a man who had committed a relatively minor offense (2 Sam. 12:5).
   b. We tend to respond most harshly to the sins we perceive in the lives of other people that are sins we are refusing to confront in our own.

IV. Her Act Was Influential (v. 3, 7-8; Mark 14:9).

Mary's act became a testimonial to her, recorded in God's Word.

A. Jesus Loved It (v. 7-8).

1. Jesus defended, affirmed, and explained Mary's actions.
   a. "But Jesus said, 'Let her alone; she has kept this for the day of My burial. For the poor you have with you always, but Me you do not have always'" (v. 7-8).

   b. "But when Jesus was aware of it, He said to them, 'Why do you trouble the woman? For she has done a good work for Me. For you have the poor with you always, but Me you do not have always. For in pouring this fragrant oil on My body, she did it for My burial. Assuredly, I say to you, wherever this gospel is preached in the whole world, what this woman has done will also be told as a memorial to her'" (Matt. 26:10-13).
2. Worship is solely for God's glory and pleasure: "For if we live, we live to the Lord" (Rom. 14:8).

B. Others Enjoyed It. "And the house was filled with the fragrance of the oil" (v. 3).

1. Though they criticized, others' lives were positively enhanced by Mary's gift of worship.
2. True worship positively enhances the lives of others around us: "God...through us diffuses the fragrance of His knowledge in every place. For we are to God the fragrance of Christ among those who are being saved and among those who are perishing" (2 Cor. 2:14-15).

C. Even More Would Hear About It.

1. Mary's story is told in three out of the four Gospels (Matt. 26:6-13; Mark 14:3-9; John 12:1-8).
   a. Mary adored; Judas became angry.
   b. Mary gave of her own possessions; Judas took from what had been given to Jesus.
   c. Mary gave genuinely and generously; Judas was a hypocrite.
   d. The disciples misjudged Mary's genuineness as wastefulness; they misjudged Judas' hypocrisy as wisdom and righteousness.

   e. Mary sacrificed a possession worth thousands for Jesus' glory; Judas squandered his entire life for his own greed.
   f. Mary's sacrifice has been upheld as a memorial to her: "Wherever this gospel is preached in the whole world, what this woman has done will also be told as a memorial to her" (Matt. 26:13; Mark 14:9).
2. God recognizes, is pleased by, and honors true worship.
   a. He memorialized Mary's worship.
   b. He has written a "book of remembrance" for those who worship Him: "Then those who feared the LORD spoke to one another, and the LORD listened and heard them; so a book of remembrance was written before Him for those who fear the LORD and who meditate on His name" (Mal. 3:16).

From sports and politics to birthdays, weddings, and Little League games, our culture doesn't hesitate to respond participatively, enthusiastically, and emotionally. When it comes to relationships, our world glorifies extravagant demonstrations of love. In comparison, how does our worship of God measure up? Do we love Jesus lavishly and continuously? Do we worship Him with hearts, minds, and spirits fully engaged? God blesses us continually with the lavishness of His love. We can return that love best by living lives of lavish worship from overflowing hearts.

1. How costly are the worship, service, time, and gifts you give toward the Lord's work? Why does God deserve the very best we have to give?

2. How much time do you spend expressing gratitude for your blessings, as opposed to time spent complaining about the challenges in your life?
3. How could nurturing an attitude of gratitude influence someone in your immediate family or circle of friends?

Worship: Welcome to Your Future

Revelation 19:1-10

When I travel, I take photographs of my family with me. Each time I look at them while I'm away, they remind me of what I have to look forward to at the end of my trip, and they increase my eagerness to reach home. Not once have I pulled out those pictures and said, "Okay, I'm satisfied. I can stay away another month."

Similarly, God has given us glimpses of what we can anticipate at the end of our journey on earth. One of these glimpses is worship. Like pictures carried on a journey, worship on earth isn't meant to satisfy but, rather, to whet our appetite and increase our thirst for what awaits us in heaven.

Heaven is a place of perfect worship. As we see God face-to-face, understand that our salvation has been completed, and realize God has made right every wrong and is firmly in control of all things, we will be compelled and enabled to worship as we've never worshiped before. We'll instantly recognize that all the worship we experienced on earth was merely a warm-up for our ultimate calling—heavenly worship.

I. Worship Will Be Prominent (v. 1-10).

A. When We Will Worship.

1. We will worship at the culmination of history.
   a. *Meta tauta*—"after this"—is a phrase used throughout the book of Revelation to indicate transition.
   b. This worship happens at the completion of the Great Tribulation.
   c. When history on earth is consummated, worship will reach its culmination.

i. All worship on earth anticipates and will reach its perfection at this event.
ii. Paul predicts: "At the name of Jesus every knee should bow, of those in heaven, and of those on earth, and of those under the earth, and that every tongue should confess that Jesus Christ is Lord, to the glory of God the Father" (Phil. 2:10-11).

2. Worship will be one of the main activities of Heaven. The everlasting gospel is to "worship Him who made heaven and earth…" (Rev. 14:7).
   a. "Whenever the living creatures give glory and honor and thanks to Him who sits on the throne, who lives forever and ever, the twenty-four elders fall down before Him who sits on the throne and worship Him who lives forever and ever…" (Rev. 4:9-10).
      i. The twenty-four elders are representatives of all the people of God—perhaps representing the twelve tribes of Israel and the twelve disciples of Jesus.
   b. "I heard the singing of thousands and millions of angels around the throne and the living beings and the elders. And they sang in a mighty chorus…" (Rev. 5:11-12, NLT).
   c. "Then I saw another angel flying in the midst of heaven, having the everlasting gospel to preach to those who dwell on the earth—to every nation, tribe, tongue, and people—saying with a loud voice, 'Fear God and give glory to Him, for the hour of His judgment has come; and worship Him who made heaven and earth, the sea and springs of water'" (Rev. 14:6-7).

B. **Who We Will Worship.** We will worship God alone.

1. We will worship the Lamb: "Let us be glad and rejoice and give Him glory, for the marriage of the Lamb has come..." (v. 7).
2. We will worship only God.
   a. John mistakenly tried to worship an angel, probably thinking it was Jesus: "And I fell at his feet to worship him..." (v. 10).
   b. The angel corrected John: "See that you do not do that! I am your fellow servant, and of your brethren who have the testimony of Jesus. Worship God!" (v. 10)

C. **Why We Will Worship.** We will worship because we were created to worship God.
1. Mankind was created with a propensity to worship something higher than himself.
   a. John fell down to worship (v. 10).
   b. People all over the world—in virtually every country and culture—worship.
   c. Knowing that His creation is compelled to worship, God told the children of Israel: "Take heed, lest you lift your eyes to heaven, and when you see the sun, the moon, and the stars, all the host of heaven, you feel driven to worship them and serve them..." (Deut. 4:19).
2. Mankind was created to have relationship with God.
   a. Rebuking people for worshiping idols, Paul said, "And He has made from one blood every nation of men to dwell on all the face of the earth...so that they should seek the Lord, in the hope that they might grope for Him and find Him, though He is not far from each one of us; for in Him we live and move and have our being..." (Acts 17:26-28).
   b. Solomon wrote, "[God] has put eternity in their hearts..." (Eccl. 3:11).

II. Worship Will Be Magnificent.

We will worship exuberantly and loudly. We will say *alleluia* (praise the Lord) and celebrate a wedding: the marriage of Jesus Christ and the church. The occasion is a joyful, long-awaited one.

A. **We Will Celebrate God's Salvation.** "After this, I heard the sound of a vast crowd in heaven shouting, 'Hallelujah! Salvation is from our God. Glory and power belong to Him alone'" (v. 1, NLT).

1. God saves us in three ways.
    a. He saves us from the penalty of sin when we accept Christ into our lives.
    b. He saves us from sin's power over our lives.
    c. He will ultimately save us from the very presence of sin—which will take place on the day of this celebration.
2. Our salvation is abundant.
    a. It is satisfying: It saves us from eternal separation from God.
    b. It is abundant: "He who did not spare His own Son, but delivered Him up for us all, how shall He not with Him also freely give us all things?" (Rom. 8:32)
    c. No other religion comes close to offering the salvation we're promised by God.
3. Salvation requires brokenness—not perfection—to be received.
    a. "God is looking for worshipers. And if the religious elite are too proud or too busy to learn to worship Him, then God seeks the worship of those whose lives are trapped in moral ruin." (Dr. Erwin Lutzer, Moody Memorial Church).
    b. Broken people recognize their need for grace and inability to be made acceptable to God by their own power.

B. **We Will Celebrate God's Retribution.** "'For true and righteous are His judgments, because He has judged the great harlot who corrupted the earth with her fornication; and He has avenged on her the blood of His servants shed by her.' Again they said, 'Alleluia!'" (v. 2)
   1. The "great harlot" is the "Babylon" spoken about in previous chapters—an economic and religious conglomerate that deceives the world.
   2. God will judge Babylon justly and harshly: "Now I saw heaven opened, and behold, a white horse. And He who sat on him was called Faithful and True, and in righteousness He judges and makes war" (v. 11).
      a. God will avenge all wrongs and reward righteousness.
      b. This is God's answer to the cry of those martyred during the tribulation: "How long, O Lord, holy and true, until You judge and avenge our blood on those who dwell on the earth?" (Rev. 6:10)
      c. This is the ultimate fulfillment of God's promise: "I will render vengeance to My enemies, and repay those who hate Me" (Deut. 32:41).
   3. God's vengeance frees us to worship Him through loving others.
      a. Vengeance is not our job: "Beloved, do not avenge yourselves, but rather give place to wrath; for it is written, 'Vengeance is Mine, I will repay,' says the Lord" (Rom. 12:19).
      b. Instead, we are to treat others with care: "Therefore, if your enemy is hungry, feed him; if he is thirsty, give him a drink; for in so doing you will heap coals of fire on his head" (Rom. 12:20).
      c. In caring for others, we worship Christ: "And the King will answer and say to them,

'Assuredly, I say to you, inasmuch as you did it to one of the least of these My brethren, you did it to Me'" (Matt. 25:40).

C. **We Will Celebrate God's Dominion.** "And I heard, as it were, the voice of a great multitude, as the sound of many waters and as the sound of mighty thunderings, saying, 'Alleluia! For the Lord God Omnipotent reigns!'" (v. 6)
   1. Evil will be defeated.
   2. Jesus will rule over all: "And I looked, and behold, in the midst...stood a Lamb as though it had been slain...Then He came and took the scroll out of the right hand of Him who sat on the throne" (Rev. 5:6-7).
      a. The Lamb is Jesus Christ.
      b. The scroll is the deed to the earth.

Worship is our appropriate response to God from the core of our being, whereby we place God above all else. A worshiper is a sinner who has recognized a need for salvation, realized that we cannot save ourselves, and accepted God's gift of salvation. Heaven will be filled with worship and worshipers. By living lives of worship on earth, we prepare ourselves for a natural transition—the ultimate graduation—into heaven.

1. Can you remember a time before you were saved that you felt you needed to worship? What caused that desire? Why do you suppose you had it then?

2. Would you describe your worship as active or passive? Do you truly involve yourself in worship or do you merely observe others doing it?

3. Does the knowledge that God will eventually correct all wrongs and punish all evil evoke a worshipful response in you? Why?